How to Keep a Work-Life Balance

Don't Neglect Your Physical and Mental Well-Being

By:

Anne Pelland

Disclaimer

authoritative information in regard to the subject matter covered and is presented solely for motivational and informational purposes only.

Nothing in this book is a substitute for medical advice nor is it intended to diagnose, treat, cure or prevent any illness or health condition. If you have a condition or health problem, consult your personal health care provider. This book is sold with the understanding that neither the author nor the publisher is engaged in rendering professional services.

Table of Contents

INTRODUCTION

Workplace-related burnout is a common problem. This is usually the result of tension in the workplace. They also feel as if they are emotionally and mentally drained when an employee suffers from work-related burnout. In addition to this, feeling true physical exhaustion is also quite normal. When this common experience appears in the life of an individual, they may be overwhelmed by a general sense of apathy. They may feel discouraged and lack the motivation to fulfill even their fundamental obligations. You'll gain an understanding of the workplace burnout here.

It is a disorder that has developed over time when a person has undergone work-related burnout. An employee is unlikely to get hit by burnout overnight. Mostly, this is a slow process that is gradually changing as time progresses. This is a direct result of stress in the workplace.

Deadlines, coping with uncooperative bosses, adverse working conditions, and working atmosphere personal unhappiness can all contribute to burnout. This disorder can affect all aspects of the life of an individual-job performance, workplace relationships, personal relationships, and even the wellbeing of an individual.

Understanding Burnout

Burnout is a state of disorder in which fatigue, exhaustion, or irritation is felt as a result of an intense focus on or commitment to a target, cause, lifestyle, or relationship that does not yield the desired reward. In other words, a burnout formula is available: expectations divided by a reality that, irrespective of the effort you spend, does not meet your expectations, is equivalent to burnout. Among hard work and burnout, there is no direct correlation or relationship. Nevertheless, there is a direct relationship or association between hard work that provides little or no benefit, and burnout. Indeed, many people are working towards exhaustion, and they are achieving recognition, recognition, and reward. Burnout is not part of the equation for these people.

Do I Have A Burnout?

Burnout is a burning slow. Burnout is not an occurrence; it is a process. Burnout is erosion-like. One day, under the waterfall, you see a huge boulder. You come back one day and half of its original size. Then it's turned into a small stone one day; then a pebble. Burnout is an internal degradation that is subtle and pernicious.

- Early burnout signs include a deep sense of fatigue, fatigue, or exhaustion that tends to stretch from your skin's surface through the tissues, ligaments, muscles, and deep into your bones and into the very cells of your body. Emotionally, at or near the end of your mental thread, you feel like you are. Psychically, you experience a sense of despair, helplessness, hopelessness, disappointment, skepticism, or anger in a world of negativity. Relationships in and out of work are struggling, they are becoming exhausting; they are no longer fun and friendly. The job becomes an endeavor on its own. It is difficult to focus on. It is a daunting challenge to stay focused. You feel and become disconnected, perhaps even unattached to your life's work and people.

- Burnout, in the end, expresses itself as an "uncareful" about life in general, about work life, family life. In the end, the energy of indignation, or rage, or disappointment cannot even be gathered; there is no energy, ever. No mental, financial, physical, psychological or spiritual feelings at any point. Just an adornment. Exhaust. Exhaust. Living alone. It's going to be a huge effort.

- Curiously, burnout affects people who once felt young, happy, enthusiastic, juicy, passionate, and incredibly curious about life and life. The result is their intention, passion, and effort to achieve unattainable goals in the process that destroyed them.

- Organizations as the burnout cause too often people think they are the sole burnout cause. They feel that they are somehow at fault because they are unable to achieve work-life balance or harmony in their way of living, or because they are unable to plan, organize, prioritize, schedule and execute, or because they are striving to be a 10 on a scale of 1-10, in everything they do, or because they are working for a manager whose expectations are too high and demanding. Individuals can sometimes be their own worst enemy and cause their burnout. Yet, not all of the time.

- Nevertheless, recent research shows that corporations and organizations are often one of the worst causes of burnout. Burnout is often incorporated into the structure of the organization today. How so? Some of the organizational characteristics that contribute to burnout are: unrealistic goals, numerous layers of bureaucracy and just-plain-stupid policies and procedures, lack of clarity in roles and responsibilities, blurry and contradictory priorities, repetitive and pointless meetings, and a mere "this is a business" mindset that focuses on people as functions while keeping the "human element" out of the equal

- And, at work, people start feeling burnout when they believe they're in a "no-win" situation-they're never going to achieve it regardless of how long and how hard they're going to work. Burnout arises when "impossible" and "irrational" writing on the wall reads, when there is no truthful or reasonable justification for the way business is conducted, the way objectives are established, the way goals and outcomes are calculated, the ambiguity of positions. When there is no link between hard work and seeing real light at the end of the tunnel (i.e. outcomes as well as "light" as in the form of "thinking," "right action" and "meaning"), people are desperate, delusional, and cynical.

- The work-related burnout is associated with many signs and symptoms. You must gain an understanding of these signals if you are in charge of employees. If you are a workplace employee, the signs and symptoms associated with burnout should also be learned. The faster you realize that burnout is obvious, the better you can work to solve the problems you face. Many of the most common signs and symptoms associated with this common and every real problem are listed below: one of the first signs of burnout is when an individual becomes frustrated. This frustration can be directed towards others, or towards the company they work in.

- The second sign that an employee may do a burnout is when their performance begins to fall apart. This sign may be the most obvious in many cases. A once-reliable person who has completed work in a timely fashion displaying a high level of quality may begin to take longer tasks to complete, and the quality of their work may rapidly decline.

- Many individuals who experience burnout in the workplace can begin to express the fact that in their work situation they feel as if they are "trapped." This is a bad sign if an individual feels "trapped." Being happy and content with the work we do is crucial. If we feel anything other than this, it is important to seek help as the burnout in the workplace becomes apparent.

- Those who experience this common work-related issue may begin to break away from friends, relatives, coworkers, social situations, and more. It is not a good sign of social detachment. This is particularly true when a person is not normally isolated from others socially.

- Many who experience burnout in the workplace may seem highly irritable. This can be seen in fast moods and similar situations. If there is no obvious cause for this type of change of personality, the problem may be linked to changes in the workplace.

- Most people may feel as if their current situation has no hope. They can walk in and out of every single day and feel a lack of motivation; many people can witness this behavior in the workplace and realize it is uncharacteristic of the individual. This is a likely sign of burnout associated with work.

- When you are feeling like you have absolutely no power, you don't get anywhere, and you are continually fed on negative thoughts and emotions, you may be experiencing burnout in the workplace.

- Most people who experience burnout also begin to experience the most different types of failures. Such mistakes may be directly related to their work performance, or in their personal life, they may be encountered.

- There is a number of causes that can lead a workplace-related person to experience burnout. A form of work-related stress may be associated with the following reasons:

Most people set their expectations too high in the workplace. Setting high expectations or making certain targets too high in the workplace is a common factor in burnout in the workplace.

- Some people may feel like they're trapped in a particular job because they can't afford a career change, or they can't pass on the advantages that a job brings. Burnout in the workplace can be felt for these people.

- Many individuals who have shown themselves to be trustworthy and provide high-quality work may be expected to regularly request additional work in addition to their normal duties. While the fact that they are given more work flatters many, this work can often become draining.

- Many are not troubled by their jobs personally. This type of work can get boring, and a person may not feel like they've got something to look forward to. This can also result in burnout in the workplace.

Organizational Strategies For Burnout Prevention

Often, the program itself is not conducive to self-care. The level of stress encountered by an employee is not always understood or consulted by managers and supervisors. Perhaps they are under tremendous pressure. If you are lucky enough to have a boss/administrator who is concerned with the employee staff's needs, here are some ideas that they might consider helping the staff.

- To disperse difficult patients and tasks, rotate staff as much as possible.
- Include workers in rotational meetings and ideas for stress relievers.
- Creating community cohesiveness through regular workouts, meetings, in-services Let staff suggest topics.
- Encourage support from peers.
- Offer recognition and excellence for success.
- Vary the responsibilities of the profession.
- We also enjoy a monthly newsletter with updates and kudos.
- Let the staff know that asking for a "stress break" is appropriate.

- Watch for signs of significant stress in the workplace and assist them.

Request for and acceptance of support must be part of the organization's community. It must be acknowledged and not seen as a sign of weakness to confess to being overwhelmed. It takes time to build the mindset needed to bring about this level of openness. Although managers may see these recommendations as overwhelming at first, their efforts will soon be rewarded with lower staff turnover, fewer days of absenteeism, more efficient and happier employees, and better patient care.

Helping Ourselves Prevent Burnout

If you are employed in a situation where administrative help is not available, you must do what you can to avoid burnout, both as a person and with your colleagues. There is often a high turnover of employees in cases where there is a shortage of administrative support. This creates increased responsibility and increased stress on the remaining assistants. Building a positive cohesive group makes it harder and raises worker's burnout.

Helping people need to learn how to take care of themselves; then it's much easier to say! Even though the helping professions today have more men the vast majority are still women in healthcare. The sense of self of women is often one of caretakers and caretakers, and this view is perpetuated by our society. Nursing and caring for women in general and nurses in particular, have been linked for a long time. Empathy is a pillar of the professions that support, particularly the "professions of women" such as nursing and social work. Historically, nurturance has been associated with and regarded as a significant nursing role. Nursing was named "professional nursing practice."

When a woman has to choose between caring for herself and caring for another, social pressure causes others to choose to nurture. Faced with what may seem like a continuous choice of caring for others or caring for oneself, women often experience conflict. It's not unusual for women to find it hard to say no or set limits, so they end up doing more than they want. They often nurture everyone but themselves with a consequential feeling of conflict, disappointment, resentment, and burning out. As women, nurses are already struggling with these issues, which are further exacerbated by the nurturer's nursing role.

Preventing Burnout.

You may feel like you're having a kind of burnout at this point, or maybe you're on your way to a stage of burnout or disinterest in your career. Don't worry, you can tackle this thinking in many ways and avoid burnout feeling.

Reduce working hours.

People who experience burnout are often those who work more than 40 hours a week. Over a long period, they could work 50 or 60 or even more hours. It impacts the work-life balance and may result in burnout. It is important to maintain a balance between the two. Talk with your boss to find out how the hours you work can be reduced. Even a small amount can help in the long run slowly.

Reassess your goals for work and career.

Sometimes you need to think about your job type of work and how it impacts your career goals. If you're doing extra work that doesn't suit your long-term goal, then ask yourself if you need to do that. If you're trying to do two people's work, ask yourself if you can get help with some of the work, or write it off. Sometimes the extra work that you do isn't as significant as it's made out to be.

Healthy eating and drinking.

A good way to reduce tension and potentially avoid burnout is to make sure you eat a balanced diet. It is also a good idea to drink plenty of water throughout your day.

Take a vacation.

Taking a vacation is one of the easiest ways to avoid burnout in the workplace. Escape the stresses of your work and take a break to a different place. It might be an offshore holiday or a trip to another country. It might be a short weekend away, or a trip to several countries for two months. It's up to your budget and time constraints, but it's a great way to recharge yourself, and when you get back you will feel refreshed.

Get enough nightly sleep.

It may seem simple, but make sure you get enough sleep every night to ensure that your mind and body are relaxed, healed, and ready to take up work on the next day.

Try to keep your work and personal life separate.

Mixing your job with your home life is a major part of the road to burnout in the workplace. It means taking home work, thinking about work while you're out, and working long hours and weekends to make things happen. While you may need to put extra hours for a project or a deadline at times, this should be the exception rather than the rule. Get into a habit of splitting your life's two zones.

What's Stress?

Stress refers to the pain caused by the conflict between our external environment and us, resulting in physical and emotional distress. It is impossible to live without stress in our fast-paced world, whether you're a student or a working adult. Positive as well as negative stress depends on the specific interpretation of the tension between the two forces by each person. It's not all negative work. Positive stress, for example, also known as eustress, may help a person work at optimal efficiency and effectiveness.

It is therefore obvious that some form of positive stress will bring to our lives more color and vibrancy. For example, the existence of a deadline will motivate us to make the most of our time and make it more efficient. It is crucial to keep this in mind, because stress management refers to the use of stress to our benefit, not to remove tension in our lives.

On the other hand, the mental and physical strain may result from negative stress. The patient may experience symptoms such as anxiety, headaches, irritability, and heart palpitations in extreme cases. Thus, while some stress can be seen as a motivating force, it is important to manage levels of stress so that it does not adversely affect your health and relationships.

Part of controlling your stress levels includes learning how stress can affect you both emotionally and physically, as well as determining whether you are functioning at your optimum stress level (OSL) or experiencing negative stress. That information will help you identify when you need to take a break or maybe look for professional assistance. It's also your first step in improving stress management strategies.

Modern pressures of the day can take the form of monetary or emotional frictions. Job pressure and increased workload can also lead to higher stress levels. How do you determine if you have excessive stress? Commonly experienced psychological symptoms include anxiety, headaches and a lack of focus. Physical symptoms are in the form of palpitations of the heart, breathlessness, excessive sweating, and stomach.

Types Of Stress

1. Acute stress.

The most severe form of stress is acute stress. It is the immediate response of your body to a new challenge, case, or demand, and it stimulates your response to fight or flight. The body turns on this biological response as the stresses of a near-miss automobile accident, an argument with a family member, or a costly work mistake sink in.

It is not always harmful to have acute stress. It's also the experience you have in a haunted house when you're riding a rollercoaster or having a person jump at you. There should be no adverse health effects of single episodes of acute stress. They can maybe good for you, as these stressful situations give the best response to potentially stressful situations to your body and brain practice.

Severe acute stress such as stress suffered as a victim of a crime or life-threatening situation may lead to problems of mental health, such as post-traumatic stress disorder or acute stress disorder.

2. Episodic Acute Stress.

It is called episodic acute stress when acute stress occurs repeatedly. Those who always seem to be undergoing a crisis tend to experience episodic acute stress. Often, they are short-tempered, irritable, nervous. Those who are either "worried warts" or cynical or who tend to see the negative side of everything often tend to experience episodic acute stress.

For people with episodic acute stress, negative health effects remain. Changing their lifestyle may be difficult for people with this type of stress because they recognize stress as part of life.

3. Chronic Stress.

It becomes chronic stress if acute stress is not overcome and continues to escalate or last for long periods. This stress is persistent and is not going away. It can be extracted from things like:

- Poverty
- A family that is unstable.
- An unhappy marriage.
- A bad job.

Chronic stress can harm your health as it can contribute to several serious diseases or health risks, such as heart disease.

- Cancer.
- Illness of the lungs.
- Accidents
- Liver cirrhosis.
- Suicide.

What's Causing Stress

What causes stress can often be attributed to the stresses put on us by society and family. Often the time we take to get involved in a hobby is the reason we can cope with pressures put on us at certain times and it allows us to better manage our lives. I'm not suggesting that we escape from our duties and responsibilities, but I'm saying that times, when we can do what we enjoy, will allow us more stress-free time and a better quality of life at other times.

Personal problems.

Health

Aging, new disease diagnosis, and current disease symptoms or complications may increase your stress. Even if you don't have health problems on your own, someone close to you can deal with a disease or illness. That can also raise the levels of stress. More than half of caregivers report an overwhelming sense of care required by their family members, according to the American Psychological Association (APA).

Relationships.

Arguments may increase your stress levels with your partner, parent, or infant. It can be even more difficult if you stay together. Problems with other family members or household members can also cause stress to you, even if you are not directly involved.

Personal beliefs.

You may be challenged by arguments about personal, religious, or political beliefs, especially when you are unable to get rid of the conflict. Major events in life that cause your own beliefs to be questioned can also cause stress. This is particularly true if your beliefs differ from those of the people who are closest to you.

Problems of emotion.

This can weigh you down with additional stress when you feel unable to respond to someone, or you need to express your feelings but can't. Also, add to the emotional strain, are mental health conditions, including depression and anxiety. Important parts of good stress management are safe outlets for emotional release and care for mental health disorders.

Changes in life.

Instances of big life changes that can be traumatic are the death of a loved one, changing jobs, moving homes, and sending a child off to college. Only positive changes can cause a significant amount of stress, such as retirement or marriage.

Money.

Financial difficulties are a growing source of stress. Credit card debt, rent, or inability to provide for your family or yourself can place you under severe stress. Financial stress is something that almost everyone can relate to in this world, where so much emphasis is placed on what you have and what you can afford. Nearly three-quarters of Americans say finance is a source of stress in their lives, according to the APA.

Social issues

Occupation.

Evidence has shown that organizational pressure and conflict can be a significant source of stress. An estimated 60% of Americans are feeling stress related to their jobs, according to the APA.

Discrimination.

Long-term stress may result from feeling discriminated against. For example, based on your race, ethnicity, gender, or sexual orientation, you can experience discrimination. Several people face prejudice and almost every day the tension it creates.

Environment.

Chronic stress can result in unsafe communities, crime-ridden towns, and other security concerns.

Traumatic events.

People who have experienced an incident that is traumatic or life-threatening often cope with long-term stress. For example, after surviving a robbery, rape, natural disaster, or war, you can experience long-term stress. In many cases, post-traumatic stress disorder (PTSD) can occur.

PTSD is a chronic condition of anxiety caused by a traumatic event or traumatic event sequence. The median lifetime prevalence of PTSD among Veterans is about 7 percent, according to the U.S. Department of Veterans Affairs ' National Center for PTSD. Females, as well as veterans and abuse survivors, are more likely to experience the condition.

The Psychological Effects Of Stress

Our body experiences ever-increasing physiological reactions as the adrenaline in our body rises-as we begin to accumulate stress. Physiology has to do with our physical responses. For instance, a man might say, "I feel stressed. I feel stressed because of my stressful job." That's interesting because I could say to that man, "Tell me about your job." He replies, "Well, I like my job. I enjoy the people I work with, I'm well paid and I'm in a good position." If the man says that to me, I'm telling him, "Well, you have a lot of positive feelings about your job. It may be health-related. It may have to do with low self-esteem. It may have to do with his relationship. It may be guilty that he doesn't have to spend enough time with his kids. Yet stress also has to do with negative emotion.

Another example is a home-wife who claims she's depressed. She can feel bored, lonely, inadequate, powerless, exhausted, or under-stimulated. Or she might feel put down and insulted if she tries to tell her husband about these feelings and he says, "What do you have to think about?" That kind of statement is likely to make her feel even worse, so it raises her tension. Note, stress is correlated with a negative emotion and so, indeed, in all kinds of situations, we have all kinds of people feeling stressed.

Stress is highly subjective. It's all about how you view it. The stress we concentrate on in this chapter is the stress we encounter in a drama of life-that means a lot of stress. I'm referring to a body that has a lot of stress and can come about in two ways. It can happen because of a particular life incident that causes the body to flood with adrenaline, such as the car accident or the tsunami.

Or because of what I call, 'relentless stress' you may also undergo a life drama. This is an accumulation of stress that happens over time so that there is no major event, in particular, just a steady build-up. It's recurring events or negative emotions that you encounter constantly-maybe in your work or relationship. If you have a build-up of negative emotion and it goes on without a break for some time, then you're going to get stressed and the feeling is the same. It's about an accumulation of adrenalin and then a flood.

Symptoms of stress when you have an extreme level of adrenaline in your body, whether it is caused by the one event or the accumulation of events, your muscles become tighter and tighter, resulting in physiological reactions. Heart palpitations, arms, neck and shoulders are always concerned-around your neck, and shoulders you end up feeling very hunched and very tight. The muscles are also going to be an ache.

Whenever you experience stress, muscle ache, particularly in the thighs, arms, is one of the common symptoms. Because your muscles ache, your body gets tired. It's like for a long time you've been carrying heavy shopping, and you can't put it down. Even after you've put down the heavy shopping, your muscles are still anxious because they've been working and getting tighter for a long time.

It affects your breathing. Simply because your chest wall is a huge muscle, the reason your breathing changes. As our muscles become tighter and tighter, the wall of the chest becomes like a tight, rigid muscle sheet. As a result, the lungs inside this chest wall are no longer able to expand as they normally do-they only expand a little bit and therefore do not take in the amount of air you normally would take in.

The brain sends a signal to the lungs after a while, "This body needs a bit more oxygen. Please breathe a bit deeper." Outwardly, you end up sighing. This forces your chest wall to open up to a larger expansion and that's what the response (sighing) is. You seem to sigh more when you're depressed or yawn more because yawning has the same effect. Yawning is when you take the chest wall into the air and cause it to stretch. Again, these are stress symptoms.

Others will notice that when they are stressed they do not sleep well. Obviously not. When you're nervous, there's a lot of adrenaline in your system. Adrenalin's purpose is to keep you safe, to keep you alive, to protect you. You're not supposed to sleep when you're on duty, and when you're tired, you won't be able to settle down and you won't be able to sleep because your brain thinks and tests, "Where's the danger?"

You are generating more and more adrenaline as the stress increases The adrenaline you generate makes your brain think more and more, "Where's the danger?" A good analogy of this is the sentry duty meerkat. It's looking around constantly, searching for risk. That's how it becomes the brain. It wonders, "Where's the danger?" And so the real adrenaline in your body makes your brain more alert, more vigilant, more worried. Therefore, sensitive people, who always have a lot of adrenaline in their bodies, appear to be concerned. The adrenaline in their body makes their brain think, "Where is the risk?" And of course, the brain begins to think, "Oh, it could be that. It could be that." You imagine what the danger might be and the body produces more adrenaline as a result.

This condition is becoming a period of anxiety. When it continues, the nervous process will eventually break down the Parasympathetic Nervous System. The Parasympathetic Nervous System becomes so drained from attempting to restore relaxation to your body that it no longer works. So, when you're thinking about anxious thoughts, your body produces Adrenaline even when you're trying to calm down and you're trying to tell yourself-your Cortex, "No, no, no, there's no risk. It's okay. Settle down. You're going to get through this. You're a big girl. Others have experienced things like this before." That's how we're talking to each other. This is our talk of self-assurance.

But when the Parasympathetic Nervous System breaks down, even as you try to calm down, you end up producing more and more adrenaline, and that's when we have constant tension and we can't calm down anymore. That's when we first understand the painful sensation. For the first time, I'm using the term ' trauma'-that's how we act when we witness the drama of life. We're feeling the pain. Our body is filled with Adrenaline and it feels like we're in a car accident, but the car is still moving. We don't know what the result will be. That's how you feel when you're traumatized.

Other things tend to happen then, as well as all the physical reactions that your body has. The body's Autonomic Nervous System begins to collapse. The Autonomic Nervous System (ANS) is the nervous system that takes care of all the tasks we do not have conscious control over. (For example, movement-blinking and walking.) So, the Autonomous Nervous System looks after our intestines and digestion, look after our intestines and evacuation, looks after our reproductive system. These are all our body's places that continue to work without us having any conscious control over them.

But what do we begin to notice when we feel stressed, even a little stressed? We continue to have tummy upsets and these upsets become more pronounced when we have a lot of stress. Many people end up with Ulcerative Colitis or Irritable Bowel Syndrome. These are quite major problems with the intestines and intestines. If you're a little stressed or a little nervous, you may have loose stools and have a lot to go to the toilet. But if you have long-term pain, you end up with major intestinal problems and problems with the bladder.

It can affect our entire reproductive system. It is well known that her menstrual cycle can change if a woman is stressed. What we now know is that men are also very affected by stress due to the advance of medical technology. With this advance in medical technology and photography, we know that the sperm of men is highly stressed and men may experience a lot of abnormal sperm and low sperm count because their Autonomic Nervous System is being interrupted.

Our Sympathetic Nervous System (SNS) and our Parasympathetic Nervous System (PNS) are the other major parts of our Autonomic

Nervous System. These are the parts of our system that take care of the body's healing and regeneration to calm down after stress. And so as that breaks down, our body is undergoing through stress without recovering.

In sum up, the first thing that begins to happen as we encounter tension when our Autonomous Nervous System breaks down is that we have a weakening in our immune system. We've concentrated on the Autonomic Nervous System, but the other thing that happens is that our immune system breaks down. As we get more depressed, we're beginning to develop more colds, cases of flu, viruses, skin conditions, and your eczema-if you're suffering from it-may re-emerge. Perhaps the Shingles or Glandular Fever will come back.

The Importance of Serotonin

A decrease in the chemical serotonin is the next thing that happens. The serotonin is depleting when you increase the adrenaline. Serotonin is the component behind our' good feeling.' It's a large product. Serotonin is a neurotransmitter we have in our brain, and we need our serotonin to feel good and think good. Serotonin enables electrical impulses to move through our brain's millions of neurons. So a lot of serotonin is a lot of good thinking. You have a lot of dopamine and you can do a lot of brainstorming if you're with friends and you feel really good. You can get on with things because you feel really good and you are motivated to get the ideas you want to do because the increased serotonin means you can think well.

Upon Serotonin's loss, you'll find your mood falling. You become flat, despondent, unmotivated, you can't be mad, you can't be cheerful. You may still push yourself to do things that need to be done when you're feeling a lot of stress, but they don't give you any more pleasure. These are the sensations in your brain of a decreased amount of serotonin.

You're also influenced by your thought. Your reasoning is impaired as it is now starting to be unreliable. You are starting to think irrationally now. At the time, you may not realize this, but afterward, when you recover a little from the stress, you might look back and think, "I wasn't thinking rationally at that moment." Our reasoning is faulty, unreasonable and nervous. At this time, the explanation of why our thought is becoming more nervous is purely biological. This hormone is a neurotransmitter in the brain that allows electrical impulses (which are thoughts) to jump across neurons when you have a lot of serotonin. When you've lowered serotonin levels, the electrical impulses don't go so far. They can't jump in different directions, so your thinking gets stiffer, your thoughts have to go anywhere else.

Because of that, they come to a halt and that's why you feel stuck in your brain when you're feeling down. You're feeling thick. You're blocked. It's not possible to think straight. How often we say "I can't think straight" to ourselves. You don't feel like going with a job you've got to do or the next thing you've got to do - it could even be cooking a meal. You can't be bothered. These are all symptoms of Serotonin being reduced.

What happens is, sadly, that these electrical impulses must go somewhere. And so they start going around in the area of the brain they just came from, which gives a recurrent thought to the individual. That's the dwelling. This is what it is to ruminate. When we're feeling down, we dwell on things. In reality, when we feel good, we do not dwell on things. Of course, we're experiencing the same anxiety process as we focus on issues because the feeling we're having is a bad thought. Because we have a bad thought, our body is producing more dopamine and the process is going on. It is the reason why we are becoming more and more nervous with reduced serotonin and with this faulty and unreasonable thought, and our brain is rising our levels of adrenaline in our body.

Both reduced serotonin levels and impaired thought lead us to lower self-esteem. A self-esteem is a form of thought. We also think badly about ourselves, as well as feeling bad. We have ongoing thoughts on how bad we are, how useless we are, how pathetic we are, or how unselfish we are. In effect, these continuing thoughts produce more and more Adrenaline.

Seeing your hands as two platforms is a simple way to remember the interaction between serotonin and adrenaline. The left hand is the hand of Adrenalin, and the right hand is the hand of Serotonin. Also, as if these devices are a counterweight, they move up and down. Serotonin is dropping as Adrenalin rises. Yet Serotonin increases as Adrenalin decreases. It is also possible to place the label' self-esteem,' on the right hand. Your serotonin and self-esteem are closely linked, and both are strongly influenced by Adrenalin's involvement.

You might have a pleasant day with mates, for example. You feel good when you get there. Your serotonin is strong, you feel good about yourself, and you feel good about life. You're not feeling stressed at all. The next day, with the same colleagues, you might be planning a dinner party. When you plan the dinner party, things go a little wrong and you realize out you didn't put the wine in the refrigerator, you didn't have enough meat and the potatoes you wanted to put on the grill turned out to be rotten. The stress is rising, the levels of adrenaline are increasing, you feel stressed, and your levels of serotonin are now decreasing. Because of that, you begin all the ruminating thoughts of, "Oh, I'm so hopeless. I should have done that before. Why haven't I checked? I'm hopeless to organize barbecues and my friends won't be happy, and they probably won't even turn up anyway".

All these needless, negative thoughts you've received are simply due to the chemical imbalance. Our stress is so affected by the way we think and once we realize this and visualize it, we can work out that if we can change the way we think, if we can change the way we see a situation and change our point of view of it, we will change the way we feel. Anything happens to us in life, we are responsible for the way we feel. We can manage our stress levels and by changing the way we feel we can work out what we're going to do next.

Understanding the Art of Stress Management

At different stages of their lives, most people in the world feel the tension. Stress occurs as a consequence of events or conditions viewed by a person as obstacles. The assumption that such challenges are unable to deal with leads to tension. Depending on the situation and how people perceive it, stress can be large or small. It can be graded according to the level of difficulty the individual faces and the level of anxiety this causes. In these types of stressful situations, some people may feel helpless and hopeless, while others may also learn the art of recognizing circumstances and ways of managing stress.

The first thing to think is the main or real cause behind the tension while in a stressful situation. There are often similar challenges surrounding that lead to stress, but identifying and concentrating on the main cause is crucial. Simplification and solution to this primary cause of stress will eventually release stress, and it becomes easy to take care of the other minor contributing factors. Once the chief stress that triggers motivation is apparent, the next step is to think about the enormous amount of pressure and stress that people around the world are experiencing. There are situations in which it is impossible even to have a simple living. If one contrasts his cause for stress with these factors, in the initial step itself, some amount of stress will certainly decrease. The next step is to tell yourself that "you're NOT alone!" because as someone thinks about the stress that other people are facing, you should also think that no one is facing a particular kind of problem situation in this world alone. There are thousands of people facing similar stress that causes problems. Finally, the self-motivating part of realizing that if people with even lower resources face their difficulty, it is certainly possible for others as well. Tools can include trusted people around us, things that can inspire us, and things that can solve our dilemma.

The fact that nature does not differentiate between people is another reason to feel stress-free. Usually, for example, when the sun shines, it provides impartial, equal for all individuals, heat and light energy to a particular region. People should learn to make positive use of the available resources to overcome their challenges in the simplest way possible without creating any stress or anxiety. When such pressures that creates challenges are overcome, a person not only feels secure and safe but also becomes trained and mentally strong in the future to face such difficult situations. It becomes especially important here that when in stressful situations a person should not only seek help from close friends and relatives but should also share his experiences with them when one successfully addresses these issues. This can motivate them with patience and strength to clear their obstacles.

Ways to Increase Productivity in the Workplace

A small business has nothing more valuable than its workers. If your workers are satisfied, they can improve their productivity, which is just what you need to help your business grow.

Small changes in behavior will dramatically improve the business ' productivity levels and office quality. This will allow you to achieve more quality work in a shorter period and reduce the amount of time spent on unnecessary tasks.

Here are top tips on how to make the most of your workers and ensure maximum productivity is maintained:

Be Efficient.

Consider how your business operates at the moment and be open to the potential to change your way of working. Note that short-term and long-term lists are just as important as prioritizing activities, especially in a small business.

Is there a better way for employees to organize their day to enable them to achieve their daily goals? Provide a schedule for each staff member and urge each to make a list to ensure that prioritized tasks are completed on time and that they stay on the job all day, resulting in productive work.

Take care of the biggest challenges when you're most alert

We often push away big goals because we're not sure we're going to achieve them... And when we get to them, we're too burnt out of our day to give them the attention they deserve. That's how tasks end up running in extra days, making it feel like productivity is gone.

Learning when and how best to work is key to getting those big projects done on time. No set schedule works for everyone... if you're an individual in the morning, first tackle your day's big tasks.

Delegate.

Delegation comes with an element of risk, but it is necessary to increase accountability to boost the staff's morale and job satisfaction. Offer responsibilities to qualified employees with a proven track record of success in a particular field and trust that they will perform the tasks well.

When you allow employees to gain skills and experience in leadership, it will support the company and give your employees a sense of accomplishment and direction in their careers.

Take Breaks For Exercise.

According to a research in the Journal of Occupational and Environmental Medicine, the use of work-time to exercise will help improve productivity. Build in set times during the week to take a walk or go to the gym, if possible. It could be just what you need to get your blood pumping to clear your head and get your focus back.

Reduce Distractions.

Social media can be a huge killer of efficiency, so enforcing a no-phone policy is not realistic. Alternatively, try to focus and involve employees while allowing them to breathe space.

Encourage all staff to turn off their mobile phones, but take regular breaks to check their phones. This will increase the productivity of the time spent at their desks.

Operating at Intervals Of 90 Minutes.

Researchers have found elite performers (athletes, chess players, musicians, etc.) who are more productive in intervals of no more than 90 minutes than those who work 90 minutes-plus. We also found that top performers tend to work no more than 4.5 hours a day. For me, it sounds good!

Have the right equipment and tools.

It is important to provide employees with the right tools and equipment for effective and timely performance of their duties. There's nothing more counterproductive than waiting for paperwork to be printed because you don't have a quick printing device.

High-quality, modern programs and equipment not only make a huge difference to the workforce, but also to the perception of your company. Using devices such as an MFP that can act as a printer, scanner, copier and fax machine to save time and effort.

Take A Nice Look At Yourself.

Some research shows that it can increase productivity by up to 15 percent by equipping an office with aesthetically pleasing elements— like plants. Jazz up your office space with a smile on your face with photos, candles, roses, or anything else.

Improve Conditions In The Workplace.

Between 68 and 70 degrees F (20-21 C) is a comfortable working temperature. An area that is too hot or too cold distracts from focus because workers are going to spend more time walking around for their jackets or an electric fan. Ensure that both heating and air-conditioning systems are in order when the season comes around.

Avoid Multi-Tasking.

Although we tend to think of multitasking capacity as an essential ability to increase productivity, the opposite can be true. Psychologists have found that attempting to perform multiple tasks at once can lead to lost time and productivity. Until going on to your next job, make a habit of committing to a single task.

Providing Support and Setting Realistic Goals.

A common problem for the managers is not having a clear, strong sense of the high-performance or not of their employees.

Need an opportunity for your staff to stay on track? Support them by achieving achievable goals. Provide managers and staff with specific guidance to help explain goals. This will help their productivity increase as they will have a clear focus and clear goals.

Practice Positive Reinforcement.

Encourage, reward and inspire. Tell employees that they do a good job and challenge constructively. Most importantly, offer personal rewards to do the job well–can they have a free holiday or a free take-out coffee to work outside their roles?

To foster a sense of fulfillment and to inspire others, you can indicate one employee's performance to other staff. If you inspire your employees to work harder and receive rewards in return, they are more likely to top their to-do list with increased productivity.

Take Advantage Of Your Commute.

Use this time to search some files, create your daily to - do list, or do some brainstorming instead of Candy-Crushing or Facebooking.

Make Sure The Employees Are Happy.

There will be no results from a stressful workplace. Workers who operate constantly in highly stressful conditions are found to be less productive and have higher levels of disengagement and absenteeism... they must be happy!

It is gratifying-and often overlooked-to show employees how much they appreciate, respect and value the company on a personal level.

Try out some of these tips and enjoy the benefits if you want your staff to work to the best of their ability.

Give Up On The Illusion Of Perfection.

Hanging on to trying to complete a job is normal for entrepreneurs— the truth is nothing is ever flawless. Instead of wasting time chasing this idea, bang your job to the best of your ability and step forward. Completing the assignment and getting it off your plate is better; if appropriate, you can always come back and later change or strengthen it.

Tips to Improve Your Health and Your Life

More people are searching for the magic solution in this day and age to improve their health and life. Hopefully, there's going to be a magic potion to make things better. If it were that easy, everyone would be in top form and their lives would be as happy as they wanted it to be.

Sadly, this is not the way life works. People can take remedies and pills to help improve overall health, but we still need to do other things to help things along. Nonetheless, we must put some effort into this, and sometimes it can be a bit daunting.

To our wellbeing, exercise is one of the most important things we can do. Walking our bodies for at least 30 minutes a day will help keep our heart healthy, maintain our weight, combat many illnesses, and help us lead a long and prosperous life. Adding weight training to our routine would help build and maintain muscle tone, making our metabolism optimum.

This allows us to burn calories at a higher rate and avoid excess weight in the harbor. It can add to the risk of some disease by carrying extra weight and make us feel tired and weak. We might not be able to carry out the daily tasks as easily as if we were fit.

Exercise increases vitality and self-esteem to be successful in our lives and the lives of our friends.

It is also a very important part of a healthy life to eat a healthy diet of fruit, vegetables, lean protein and whole grains. Eating many small meals a day will help maintain the energy levels throughout the day on an even keel. Through eating every few hours and keeping it light and safe, stop the mid-afternoon crash. If it's difficult to eat that often you might want to consider adding a protein shake to your daily diet.

Many people find it helpful to supplement their diet with dietary supplements. Taking vitamin and mineral supplements will help fill the gap if one hundred percent of the recommended daily allowance is not provided to us by our diets. These can help us feel more healthy and alert, and they can help to reduce the risk of certain diseases.

The important factor that needs to be considered and that seems to be most ignored is to keep tension at bay. Relax and refocus yourself and just enjoy your life. Try to improve places that cause stress in your life. This may include relieving your workload or getting help from someone. Perhaps just getting out for time alone with your significant other will give you a much-needed break from the stresses of day to day at home. Meditation can be a good way of anxiety as well.

We need to take steps in our own hands and make choices that are healthy and safe for us and our family to improve your health and your life. To track your progress and see where improvements can be made, keep a daily food, exercise and stress log.

CONCLUSION

Burnout in a workplace is a common issue that needs to be addressed. It is important to know and understand the basics of burnout in the workplace if you are in charge of employees. If you're an employee, knowing and understanding the basics is also critical. You will combat work-related burnout by knowing the conditions that cause this to happen, the symptoms associated with the condition, and how to resolve it!